Québécité

Québécité

A JAZZ FANTASIA IN THREE CANTOS

George Elliott Clarke

GASPEREAU PRESS PRINTERS & PUBLISHERS MMIII

Geraldine Elizabeth Clarke (1939–2000)

&

Lillian Liu Jackson (1937–1995):

Two Dreamers of Beauty

Her Excellency The Right Honourable Adrienne Clarkson

&

The Right Honourable Pierre Elliott Trudeau (1919–2000):

Two Visionaries of Liberty

Ce qui n'est pas beau a tort d'être;
La beauté n'aime que la beauté….
La beauté est la seule chose qui n'existe pas à demi.

HUGO

Poetry wafts, swafts, *over obstacles of paper,*
So pages unfold, dissolve, resolve into Verse—
Whatever you're singing now.
Every word must be Song, but sans *rehearse….*

Perhaps the answer was in the songs.

BALDWIN

Prelude

> *La littérature mène à l'amour,*
> *l'amour mène à la littérature.*
> LEDUC

This "libretto" is for connoisseurs. Its stanzas were sculpted of the aggravated *gravitas* of Miles Davis's trumpet, the salacious solace of James Brown's howls, the fearless *laissez-faire* of Oscar Peterson's piano, and the oceanic *négritude* of Portia White's contralto. I confess: it is also a callaloo confection—or gumbo concoction—of Alfred Hitchcock's *I Confess* (1953), Marcel Camus's *Orfeu Negro* (1959), Jacques Demy's *Les Parapluies de Cherbourg* (1964), Spike Lee's *Mo' Better Blues* (1990), Mira Nair's *Mississippi Masala* (1991), Clement Virgo's *Love Come Down* (2000), and Sanjay Leela Bhansali's *Devdas* (2002). Given these traditions, plus my own tendencies, eccentricities, affinities—lugubrious, lubricious, lubricated—this production accepts that History is a slaughterhouse, Poetry an opera house: only Love allows us to distinguish Beauty from its extinguishing.

The rainbow quartet of lovers presented here enacts no allegory. These personae are *Fashion File* models of rhetorical ambition—chameleon chiaroscuro, erotic chintz, coarse discourse, Romanticist sado-canticles. Their sung speech is an avenue of sonnets leading to (and fleeing from) the Eden—Golgotha-like—of sex. Their story is set in Ville de Québec because its architecture is Gothic, its vices baroque. Too, Québec is a cinema of words, a cathedral of jazz, a catwalk of politics, a theatre of art, a *fête* of nostalgia, a gallery of passion, and a theme park of dreams. It offers us curried caribou, neon haiku, chanted blues.... Poco, pomo, it is a refuge from desiccated aesthetics.

Thus *Québécité* is an Absinthe-Amarula-Brandy-Champagne-Chartreuse-Chicoutai-Cognac-Grappa-Palm-Port-Pastis-Rum-Saki-Sangria-Scotch-Tequila-Vodka opera, one coloured spicily with notes of ebony, dark-cherry, India indigo ink, and bronze-beige the shade of papyrus or bamboo. If possible, your eyes must savour lilies here—lilies laced in licorice; your ears must accept African strings, Asian brass, European percussion, Aboriginal vocals.

Yes, the word *love* is bastardized in every language. But hear Provençal's Mistral: "*Lou soleu me fait cantar*." And—look!—light gilds the sky.

GEORGE ELLIOTT CLARKE
Toronto, Ontario, June 2003

Québécité

WARNING: THIS WORK MAY BE, EVEN IN CANADA,
SUNG LOUDLY—AND WITH FEELING.

It takes a barbarian to recognize
the fallibility and splendor
of a capital

P.D. SCOTT

No matter what Bourassa or Parizeau or
any of them say, we are Quebecois.

GALE

Dramatis Personae

LAXMI BHARATI

Université Laval student architect, 21. Hindu, of Indian descent, born and raised in Montréal.

COLETTE CHAN

Université Laval law student, 21. Of Chinese origin, she escaped the 1989 'Goddess of Democracy' pogrom.

OVIDE RIMBAUD

Haitian, of black-white ancestry, brought to Québec by his parents in 1989. A Ville de Québec-based architect, 25.

MALCOLM STATES

Montréalais jazz saxophonist of African-American and Mi'kmaq Nova Scotian heritage, debuted in Halifax. An Africadian, he's 25.

Musicians: A-J, *piano;* SANS SOUCI, *bass;*
BLUE, *drums;* SEPT-ÎSLES, *trumpet.*
(Other personnel may be drafted as required.)

The Scene: Fin de xxe siècle
Ville de Québec, Vieux-Québec.

Priveliged group of people. Debate love through architectural metaphors.

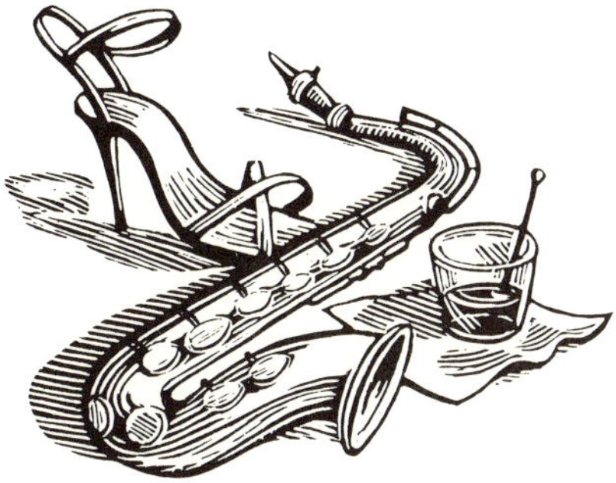

Canto I

Sacrum, sacrum, inluminatio coitu.

POUND, CANTO XXXVI

Scene i: Devant Le Château Frontenac

Flamboyant stage directions.

[*In a blue-lilac dusk ignited by light petals of rain, the very pollen of cream-blossomed April,* OVIDE *holds a black velvety umbrella. He is dandy in a candy-pink shirt, mauve jacket, and natty black pants. A gold crucifix dangles from the gold chain girding his neck. Wearing a French chiffon gold and turquoise sari, and holding a mirroring umbrella,* LAXMI *faces her wanna-be amadou. (Her look is sandalwood-infused ivory. Her earrings, are they excited, Golconda diamonds?) The pair stands on la terrasse Dufferin before the fantabulous, Gothic-styled Château Frontenac. Grey gargoyles jut from a low roof, but cream-flesh-coloured blossoms arc upwards to meet them—as if in love. A bass commixes with church bells chiming in bluesy discord.* OVIDE *gestures at a flowering, glowering tree.*]

O: Laxmi, when apple blossoms blaze,
Name them beautiful;
Feel the vivid warmth of Love—
Fleshed heat, palpable.
Will you fulfill my meaning?
Am I meaningful?

L: You've invited me to savour jazz—
Lightning born alive as chocolate....

O: *Le goût intense du vrai chocolat....*

L: Why taint it with saccharine hints,
Such sick cadence of decadence?

Is there some fault in your feelings?
Are your plans purely floors and ceilings?

O: I speak only as an architect
Bracing a Laval student architect.
I've my own firm; I'm stable, mature.
My designs are pure.

L: Only my blueprints, Ovide, should be blue.
I'll found gaudy temples, Gaudi's genius pursue.

Virtue is the steely mettle I trust:
My husband will be iron, not rust.

O: Virtue should not buckle to Vice.
(Québec's no Puritan paradise!)
But your eyes could set fire to ice.

L: To breathe Occidental oxygen,
Say my parents, is to go rotten.

So I hex all wrecks and vexations of men.
Oh, what is wrong with women is men!

O: Laxmi, you'll always be beautiful.
You're going to always be capitally beautiful—
Like Québec Cité, Québec Cité,
This rococo, Art Deco, disco city.

L: This medieval, bonfire-lit, Gothic, sleazy,
Tear-gas-tainted, politics-poisoned city,
Stained by bikers, strippers, drug violence….

O: No, no, Canadians don't like to wield guns!

L: They don't have to: they have drivers' licences.

O: Québec perfects Canadian architecture.

L: For *its* buildings *aren't* satire fused with *film noir*….
But your chat showcases built-in imperfection!

O: Lakmé, you are cinnamon-copper skin
And plum lips ablaze. Is that a sin?

L: Ovide, you're as magnetic as a collision;
But kisses are just prefaces to perdition.

O: I could scat sing my ballad valentine!

L: Just serve me *verres* of very fine wine.

O: *Je suis Haïtien*, with pure, sugar love to advance.
Let's sip chilled Haitian rum, distilled in France—
Watch petals wafting on wisps of fragrance.

L: *Non*, I just don't trust,
Don't trust Romance:

Too much is lust,
Too much is chance.

O: The bed decides
Who is competent to wed.
The bed decides
What grooms wed which brides.

L: Men crave messy, messianic, extra-satanic sex
That turns psycho, sycophantic, or pedantic next.

O: Our Virtue's verified by our tenderness.

L: Seduction is no promise of happiness:
Seduction's a satisfaction sated with pain.

O: Such gargoyle words could scare off rain—
Québécoise April's blossoming rain!

L: Ovide, I prefer Puccini with cappuccino—
Or Picasso with espresso—
To vain talk that bleeds like a vein.

So let's go hear the Malcolm States Quartet
At La Révolution Tranquille, *mon bon architecte*.

O: *Oui,* let's scat!

[Their umbrellas blossoming, the pair strolls off. Study a mosaic of piano amid a collage of saxophone—a Riopelle parleying with a Pippin.]

Scene ii: À La Révolution Tranquille

Name suggests allianment w/ Quebec souvereignty Despite ethnicity.

[In this scene it is seen that MALCOLM *hoists a saxophone to his lips. A suave man in a black suit, his crisp white shirt offset by a skinny black tie, he stands in a corner of the nightclub that a crimson fluorescent sign declares to be "La Révolution Tranquille." A poster features Malcolm in a dour pose, in dark sunglasses, standing before the equally surly "Malcolm States Quartet," featuring* A-J *on piano,* SANS SOUCI *on bass,* BLUE *on drums, and* SEPT-ÎSLES *on trumpet. The bar itself: tones of warm maple and silky grey stone. In one corner, a small shrine to Chinese ancestors and deities glows red, to summon good luck. On the walls appear early 1960s-era posters of (your choice among) Martin Luther King, Pierre Elliott Trudeau, Ho Chi Minh, René Lévesque, Fidel Castro, Oscar Peterson, Lili St-Cyr, John Coltrane, Golda Meir, Miles Davis, James Brown, Indira Gandhi, Ella Fitzgerald, Jean Lesage, Buffy Saint-Marie, Portia White (photographed by Karsh), Josephine Baker, Adrienne Clarkson, Malcolm X, Gamal Abdel Nasser, Oliver Jones, Leonard Cohen, Bruce Lee, Ravi Shankar, Astrud Gilberto, Geneviève Bujold, Nancy Kwan, and Jawaharlal Nehru. The bar is Warhol retro, with chrome and brass fixtures, and marble frills, soft-lit.]*

Decor → Shrine for ancestors + 60's posters
↳ Hybridity.

M: Imitate Holland-Dozier-Holland:
Make it hard, make it hot, make it damned.

[MALCOLM *blows scales that are piano glissades. Then he sets down the saxophone and sings.*]

M: If I was not your lover, who was?
Those days, hungry in the grass,
Your skirt, spread like an hourglass,
Butterflies mobbing us at dusk:
Baby, we are close enough to know
We are no longer close now.

[COLETTE *enters the bar. Beautiful, a fashionista, she wears a Sung white silk blouse, a pleated, paisley indigo miniskirt, flat black shoes, and her two black braids. She carries a fat law book, a pink umbrella, a cellphone, a* Le Devoir *newspaper, and a bag of clementines.* COLETTE *plunks these items on a table.* MALCOLM *motions his quartet to cease playing.*]

M: Take a break. See y'all in an hour. A'-'ight?

[*The band exits (apparently).* COLETTE *sits and begins to peel a clementine.*]

M: [*To* COLETTE.] Don't judge these harsh sounds too harshly.
Their notes echo a man who loved too brashly.

C: I study human-rights law at Laval.
I don't try to judge what's musical,

Though I courted piano as a gal.
But the law states, Mr. States,
Nothing can be done about lost love:
But no one's free who isn't free to love.

M: You speak so deliciously,
And with such cadenced balances.
You parley so judiciously,
Like spectres at séances.
If I may say so, Ms. Chan, I presume.
Please, please, please, call me Malcolm.

C: In *Franglais*—as in *joual*—my name's Colette.

M: Its accent's perfume, scented, in a novelette.

C: If only English weren't such anguish!
If only French were not so *gauche*!

M: That's Canada's anomalous calamity:
Anglos muck up the Queen's English;
Francophones fuck up French.

C: Your wit seems as politically virtuoso
As Laferrière's in *How to Make Love to a Negro*.

M: *Oui*, I chastise 'Vegas' Céline *via* Marjo,
Sample MC Solaar with Gilles Vigneault.

C: I like the legalese, neo-Chinese, of Pierre Trudeau:
Fatta la legge, trovato l'inganno.

Jurisprudence is pure Music—as Plato quotes.

M: When it's harmonious, not fissiparous notes—
sounding like fissile, fractious Canada.

C: Canada is as lovely as fine china,
but no place is as lovely as my China.

M: Why did you leave that place you love?
Was it Fear—or Love—that drove your move?

C: Bullets blasted away ballads and ballots,
and bodies were 'miscounted' everywhere:
only nobodies numbered as the dead,
when China drove us out in '89,
when I was nine.
A Communist comrade warned us
worshipping Freedom could be fatal,
so my Lincoln-minded parents,
two profs adoring forbidden Ellington,
fled with all their hidden Ellington:
our total worldly goods were Music.
Then they opened this nightclub—café,
dreaming of a Bebop-Fusion Cathay.

M: Sad I am for your strife; glad I am you've arrived.

C: Because our dreams were solely Music, we survived.

[MALCOLM *hefts* COLETTE'S *book, then sets it down.*]

M: Such tonnage must be the Law's motherlode.

C: [*Laughing.*] It's got something for everyone—
it's the *Criminal Code*.

M: Music's the code wherein Philosophy delves.

C: And laws shadow fears—their phantom selves....

How did you, Malcolm, come to the sax?
Why are you, Malcolm, ex of Halifax?

M: Halifax is a Hell of Haligonians—
And Stygian, nasty Nova Scotians.

racism. Critique of Can. nation.

To forget my regrets, I picked up piano,
but saxophone was lighter to brandish than piano.

C: Do you mind if I listen in tonight?
I have piano, violin—and...I like your sax.

M: [*Impishly.*] It's not just biology; I'm practiced.

C: [*Laughing.*] I said *sax*, not *sex*.

M: I'd love to hear your fingers minuet, Colette.
Alight by me, dove; let's début a duet.

[MALCOLM *places his saxophone on top of the piano and slides onto the piano bench.* COLETTE *wipes her clementine-wet fingers on a wet napkin, then rises to sit beside* MALCOLM. *The piano extends before them like the future.*]

C: Look! My legs are so short,
my feet can hardly touch the ground.

M: Then I'll sit close by, close, to feel each sound.

[COLETTE'S *feet dangle while she impresses the piano.*]

C: Lushly, a dewed light falls,
blushing branches.
It clears what doubts had pressed down leaves
and lets kissed lips—
lilacs, lilies, tulips—
flourish,
lushly flourish.

M: The new spring, with fresh blossoms, comes.
Lovers purr, purl, pour themselves like balm
Or ointment on each other, then fall calm,
Then sun heaps light in their eyes—like poems.

C: I must shout, sing—
Loud, liberal—

To have sweet lungs:
Plus, it's April.

M: You may be *une étudiante en droit*,
but you *are* a pianist—*si vous désiriez l'emploi*.

C: No, it's your music that resembles
beautiful, fragrant, apple blossoms.

[*Song continues anew.*]

C: The sea-green trees, the snow-white blossoms—

M: The star-stormed night, so blatant with blossoms,

C&M: Flaunt a florilegium of dazzling perfumes.

[*A clash of thunder, then shouting rain.* COLETTE *smiles at* MALCOLM, *leaps up, grabs her book, and swirls out of the bar.* MALCOLM *holds up two clementines like two crystal balls.*]

M: Ah, clementines like fine china,
lovely like fine-boned, delicate china,
these choice clementines, finely, from China.

And how can I even now not dream her sable-delectable-
hurting-flirting-vigilante-*cognoscenti*-oblique-unique-
circular-oracular-glassine-hyaline-tasty-T'ang Dynasty
Eyes?

Scene iii: Devant la basilique-cathédral de Québec

[LAXMI *and* OVIDE, *toting umbrellas, pause to contemplate the Shaker-plain cathedral. La Révolution Tranquille shimmers across the street—like an impressionist canvas by Curtis Mayfield and The Impressions.*]

O: You vaunt Virtue, and here it is, proud and pretty—
This haunting edifice that deifies Quebec City!

L: The sky is frail white stars, broken, raining.
(An honest lingo needs no explaining.)

O: Crows rise, like high notes, flashing to Heaven—
But lovers sweat, swoon, and moan.
Love is as lonely as a man and a woman
Loving each other alone.

L: Like stars—in pointed, pitted emptiness,
When will every word fit in its own place?

Between lips barely suited for words—
Because so relentlessly hard and soft—
Slip lies in gilt, gift-wrapped words.

O: Yet Love cost this much oft....

L: Let's taste cool jazz; see rum, iced, blazing, quaffed!

[*Arm-in-arm, they troop across the street and storm La Révolution Tranquille.*]

Scene iv: Blues de Malcolm

[LAXMI *and* OVIDE *sit at a table in La Révolution Tranquille. Gigantic, olive-garnished, martini glasses sit swimmingly before the pair, along with a video camera. Sound of the Malcolm States Quartet tuning up. Wearing a lime-green tennis skirt and an aquamarine blouse,* COLETTE *sits at another table. Holding his saxophone and standing at a microphone,* MALCOLM, *in an indigo suit, violet shirt, and gold tie, sings.* OVIDE *films the unfurling music.*]

M: I's gonna sing now, so silence that cellphone—
Less ya wanna get bopped hard by my saxophone!

[*Sounds of laughter, whoops, hollers, cheers, glasses tinkling.*]

Leave them damned things off! Best: leave em at home!
Ici à Quebec City, *voici "Blues de Malcolm."*

If you're down and out,
Good and Evil don't matter.
If you're down, dirty, and out,
Vice and Virtue don't matter.
But if you're up and coming,
Your innocence will shatter.

Now I go from drink to drink,
And I've gone from gal to gal.
Yes, I slip from bad to worse,
And I've fallen from gal to gal:

The ones I want promise Paradise,
The ones I get give me hell.

I ain't blue: the rain still works;
The wind hasn't broken down.
I ain't blue: the rain, it still works,
The wind ain't all fallen down.
And the sun, it still burns, it burns,
It burns right down to the ground.

[*The audience applauds.* MALCOLM *signals for a break. The band members exit (apparently).* COLETTE, *French style, kisses* LAXMI *and* OVIDE *on their cheeks.* OVIDE *films this moment, then sets his camera down.*]

C: How erect's the architecture?

L: How prospers the law?

C: The law profits the rich—as usual.

L: And we architects demolish flowers.

[*Les demoiselles laugh.*]

L: Colette Chan, do you know Ovide Rimbaud?

C: [*To* OVIDE.] You designed La Révolution Tranquille, I know.

O: *Enchanté*, Ms. Chan. Let me buy a round of rum.

[OVIDE *goes to the bar.*]

C: Laxmi, *est-ce qu'* Ovide *serait ton chum*?

L: *Pas du tout*, Colette!

C: *Pas encore, peut-être*!

[OVIDE *returns with three glasses holding three fingers of rum. The leonine* MALCOLM *approaches the table.*]

L: Ovide, your design for this place is deservedly brilliant.

O: I admire Beauty that's unreservedly resilient.

C: May I introduce Malcolm States?
Malcolm, this is Laxmi Bharati,
An architecture student at Université Laval.

M: *Je suis charmé par votre élégance.*

C: And the architect, Ovide Rimbaud, is her….

L: Acquaintance.

C: Laxmi, his name chimes handsome with romance!

O: Ovide—like the poet; Rimbaud—like the poet.

M: Poets never sound like anything but poets.

O: May I be a poet speaking to other poets?

L: The word *love* bleats and chirps in their sonnets.

O: Yet, Petrarchan sonnets *première* with Sade—
because Petrarch adored an ancestress of Sade.

L: Poets are eyes looking for eyes
to look into, eyes to inspire fresh lies.
(They are pure piranha in hyena disguise.)

C: [*Smiling.*] It's cynical to feel so clinical about emotion.

L: *Mais l'éros est comme une érosion.*

O: Poetry is endlessly fresh, like dew, like grass.

C: Love refreshes, well, like a wine-drenched glass.

M: *Je vais demander du vin.*

[MALCOLM *goes to the bar and returns with a glass of wine.*]

C: Let white wine oil oenophiles—
and black-and-white cinéphiles.

O: Eternity could not be endless without wine.

L: Love cannot be endless without scruples.
Consider conscious "Couplets for Couples":

Those who are over-sensual
Are more acting than actual.
(Their passion's biological.)
Those who are under-sensuous
Are more vain than virtuous.
(The best are tortuous.)
Do not feel less or much:
Love exceeds our sense of touch.

[*The party applauds* LAXMI. *They hold up their glasses like video cameras.*]

M: Conceivably, such couplets
  can't conceive of quintuplets.

O: Laxmi, you negate Nature, and that's unnatural.
Even nimble priests to supple *putains* tumble.

Holy, the landscape lacks all inhibition:
Wind, rain, and flowers enact ecstatic coition.

(In Vienna, near the opera house, when it's warm,
The green rows of ash trees smell just like sperm.)

L: Only harlots are heated by such rhetoric—
As are mistresses, middling, melodramatic.

O: Listen: Sin is always cinematic.

C: You're both quite talkative.

L: It's recitative.

C: Signify, Malcolm, your sizzling aesthetic of jazz:
Is it Neo-Traditional or "Free," fluid like crime stats?

M: Jazz is indelible rainbow *aquarelles*;
Jazz is nights fallen open like a dress—and just as sweet;
Jazz is saxes stroked like violins, pianos beat like drums;
Jazz is the *vice versa* of Vice and Virtue;
Jazz is multiculti-Aboriginal-Semitic-Afro-Asian-Caucasian;
Jazz is fried pigtails, mango, and *Tabasco*-splashed curry;
Jazz is Lana Ogilvie in a Jean-Michel Basquiat;
Jazz is Chinese motifs in blues with black motives;
Jazz is deluxe, diabolical, champagne-and-vodka martinis.
Jazz is the human right to Pleasure and Bauhaus-curvaceous Joy.

Jazz lives and survives:
Jazz kills executives.

O: Malcolm, your style mimics dd Jackson;
No, it's more like, *oui*, J.J. Jackson,
His 1966 hit, "But It's Alright."

M: Oscar Peterson is my idol.
De temps en temps, I dream I'm his rival.
But I also worship Portia White.

C: A *coloratura* contralto, Miss White
Divided darkness and divined the light.

L: It's late, the rain is strong, and so, good night.

C: The rain and the street lights pastel a poem.

L: *Au revoir*, Colette; *à bientôt*, Malcolm.

C: "Can any joyful leaning be obeyed,
If the desiring heart is first denied
Satisfactory love?" So Tu Fu said.

M: This scripture is sunlight inside.

O: O! Laxmi, to win your sunshine, I will sing.

L: If you don't sing well, you'll just get rain.

O: Then I'll love the rain as if it were sunlight, melting.

L: Never mistake ginger ale for champagne.

O: I'd love to take, not *mistake*, you as my missis....

L: Don't confuse Quebec City for Rome,
And don't confuse a few blasé kisses
For blazing entrée to a *baisodrome*....

[LAXMI *and* OVIDE *take their leave, leaving* COLETTE *and* MALCOLM *alone together, so sophisticatedly au naturel: two flowers aflame.*]

Scene v: Clémentines

[MALCOLM *and* COLETTE *sit at a table in the candle-lit La Révolution Tranquille. The saxophone rests atop the piano.* MALCOLM *clasps* COLETTE'S *hands in his own. A violin snoozes on the table.*]

M: Like late Lear, I'm lighthearted,
        finally humbling to Love.

C: It's too early to speak of Love.
It's too easy to speak of Love.

(Time breaks all spoken vows.
Time speaks all broken vows.)

We wrestle, we wrestle, with Life,
Then we are thrown:
Time has its way with us;
The grave has its own.

M: But to not burn for Love
Is to be ice-cold stone.

[MALCOLM *begins to play "Clémentines" on the piano.* COLETTE *accompanies on violin. She serenades 'her' pianist.*]

M: Your hair unclasps like wine,
your fingers blush to orange.

I taste your flurried moans,
sugar Aprilling lips.

Il neige sur tous les toits
after two clementines,

clement, Laurentian wine,
plush, orange-cinnamon tea....

On ne vit pas d'amour
et d'eau fraîche.

Sino-Québécoise, imago
of Beijing and Beaupré,

stitch together aubades,
monostich by monostich,

til a sudden poem whips,
thrashes, frothing your book.

C: It is so beautiful, Malcolm, I can't move.
But words, oh words, contaminate Love!

[COLETTE *begins to cry and turns away.* MALCOLM *turns her to face him. She sets down the violin. He hugs* COLETTE, *this beauty—bronze and brass—who resembles Vanessa Mae—if filmed by Tinto Brass.*]

M: Why? Why? Why?

C: Words have an annoying tendency
to turn into lies.

[MALCOLM *kisses* COLETTE. *She answers, tentatively, then voluptuously.*]

M: We'll cleave as one—then, in past tense, clove.

C: Malcolm, you could prove you love a stove!

[*Again, kisses.*]

M: Let Love, like Genesis, break night in two—
One half into rain, one half into dew.

C: I wish Love were simple. I wish many things.
But my heart is a song that Love now sings.

Scene vi: Au centre-ville, sous la pluie

[*In this scene is seen* LAXMI *and* OVIDE, *umbrellas unfurled, streaming through a pluviôse-like downpour and down a cobblestone street. They shelter in a gargoyled archway.* OVIDE *kisses* LAXMI; *she pushes him away.*]

L: You're as sophisticated as Mephistopheles,
But any hypocrite can press out kisses—
The *sine qua non* of hypocrisy.

O: *T'es sans souci, aussi un peu* sassy!
Why can't we be enlightened?
Laxmi means *light*. Perhaps you're frightened?

L: Am I to be coupled like a boxcar?
Is that what all your words are for?

O: You are so sparklingly beautiful, Laxmi,
Any poem for you must glisten like a jewel—
But still its facets must gleam facetious:
How could mere glitter compare to sunshine?

L: Such symphonic speech,
Such lyrical kisses!

O: My inspiration's Afric—
But French in places.

[*Some birds flit, squawking, overhead.*]

O: Crows caress
the wind's nape—
then undress
its thin shape.

L: The birds bicker like bitchy guitarists—
Or like tourists, those first-class terrorists....

O: I'd like to snap their necks, crush their cameras!
Still, my kisses surrender violent tenderness....

L: You seek a spasm of *amplexus* some afternoon—
A little brown sugar for your *café au lait* spoon....

I suspect you expect *Kahlùa* with milk
Guarantees feats of sex amid feasts of silk....

O: Compose free kisses like poets compose *vers libre*.

L: In Québec, there is no freedom: just read *Cité libre*—
Or its hang-em-high antagonist, *Allô Police!*

O: Laxmi, play Delibes's delicate Lakmé, please.

L: But, for Love, I'd never swallow the *dhatura*,
That pale, fatal, poisonous flower.

O: But I'd play Romeo with bravura.

L: Don't cast us as two outcast characters—
Crass as those in Baldwin's *Another Country*,
His drastically orgiastic actors,
Concocting unconscionable *cochonneries*.

O: Let us sculpt a love-nest cathedral....

L: I think you mean a *Kama Sutra* brothel!
Le Moulin Rouge is more your moral style,
Ovide, not the immaculate Taj Mahal.

[OVIDE *shakes his head 'no' and then kneels, on a dry spot, before* LAXMI. *He touches her feet.*]

O: As you pass, moon-orange
marigolds bow down in awe
at your auburn feet.

[LAXMI *turns away. She resembles Madhuri Dixit in Versace and Marpessa Dawn in* Orfeu Negro.]

L: Love is always, always, a risk.
Ah, who can I ask? Oh, who can I ask?
What is true in a kiss or embrace?
What a lover reveals is always less.

[OVIDE *stands and embraces la ravissante* LAXMI.]

L&O: Oh, these vexations will go on like hexes,
For nothing's as vexatious as the sexes
When it comes to sex.

L: Ovide, I'm no tabloid starlet—
Half Girl Guide and half coquette.
I'm a virgin—and proudly that.

O: Laxmi, your purity is a treasure,
Not plunder to loot—

L: Or pollute—

O: At leisure.

[LAXMI *lets* OVIDE *kiss her—sketchily—in the rain. Light lolls—as if drafted by Douglas Cardinal. Sound of a foghorn.*]

Scene vii: Au Château Frontenac

[*In a pink-and-gold chamber in Le Château Frontenac,* MALCOLM *and* COLETTE, *wearing white bathrobes, sit on the king-size bed.* COLETTE'S *feet don't touch the floor;* MALCOLM'S *saxophone sprawls on the bed. A gold chain circles* MALCOLM'S *neck;* COLETTE'S *gold necklace dangles a jade Buddha pendant.* COLETTE *picks up her cellphone and turns it off. Night!*]

M: Your daddy's A-1, a pure jazz aficionado,
To castle a saxman who's a handsome Quasimodo.
Le Château Frontenac is swank civility.
Does he know, does he know, you're here with me?

C: If he knew, he'd be in Hell—hellishly.

M: There's no Hell like the Christian one.
Let's sip whiskey—and scotch all sin.

[MALCOLM *opens a mini-bar, withdraws two small bottles, pours them into two glasses, and hands one to* COLETTE. *They sip, then recline on the bed and kiss.* COLETTE *sits up, plucks a book from the bedside table, holds it up.*]

C: Is Aristotle's *Poetics* your seduction guide?

M: He knows the laws about mirth and ruth.
But James Brown's cries be the *Gospel*'s truth.

You're not afraid? Are you dissatisfied?

C: My feelings … I cannot say just yet. We've kissed—
Kisses that set me reeling like a surrealist.

[COLETTE *drains her whiskey.*]

C: The key to my heart seems to be whiskey.

M: I'm always off-key—lest I have whiskey.

[MALCOLM *puts away the saxophone. He and* COLETTE *enter the bed and, under the crème-fraîche covers, doff their bathrobes.* MALCOLM *looks softly at* COLETTE, *and then softens the light. Feel here a rose-gold lamé Lagerfeld vibe.*]

M: Colette, your beauty's as natural as honey.
To portray you, sonneteers need apply
Gold paints almost too bright for flesh.

C: When I was a girl, about twelve,
Mama ushered us to a Parti Libéral *fête*—
all those Grit Quebecers kvetching,
and I wore a white sundress she bought me
that was totally, utterly, see-through,
showing everything—and no bra!
Imagine....

M: I cast you thus—like a magician:
"Abracadabra!"

[MALCOLM *removes* COLETTE'S *white unlaced corset from under the covers and casts it aside. Rain drizzles pizzicato, petulant, upon the window.*]

M: Let this night be our bed....

C: Malcolm, are you, like Casanova, callow?
Am I a morsel you'll taste and swallow
And forget...in just an ellipse—
Like a satisfied gourmet wiping his lips?

M: Colette, all my heartfelt, honest kisses
Are rich, *riche*, rigorously religious.

[MALCOLM *sits up, opens the mini-bar again, and extracts two mini bottles.*]

M: What would you like? There's *Calvados*,
Or *Cockspur* rum—from Barbados.

C: *Calvados*, then smoked oysters with smoked salmon,
Then almond pudding with croissants with almond.

[COLETTE *empties one bottle into her glass, so Cirque-du-Soleil sinuous.*]

C: Of flesh, and blood, and bone,
We are made alone.
With these same things,
We are made lonely:
The white moon only
Owns true-wed wings.

M: When that dawn sun blasts forth light,
I'll bang a tambourine.

C: Oh, I'll love you til forever—
And each day in between.

M: You're a Manet siren in a Monet scene,
A Chiang Yee vision dreamt by Anaïs Nin.

[*The lovers kiss. Darkness, an erection of flutes, then a triumph of Tijuana-flavoured trumpet braying* Olé!]

Canto II

LOVE, gone as lightning....
POUND, CANTO XCV

Too much love

Scene i: Trop d'amour

[*Bells chime out dawn. While* MALCOLM *slumbers,* COLETTE, *in tangerine bra and panties, dons a short, pink chiffon skirt and a sun-gold silk shirt, then gold knee-high stockings, and then, before a full-length mirror, a Liberal Party-red beret. She steps into lipstick-pink high heels and a fluorescent gold backpack, then kisses* MALCOLM, *who awakes, sits up, and looks into sun-wicked eyes.*]

C: Law school awaits my anarchy, *mon chéri.*

M: Careful: lawyers go to legislatures—
Or the hoosegow, just like whores.

C: And musicians? Don't they go to asylums
Or end up waxed, shellacked, in museums?

[*With flamboyant panache,* MALCOLM *pulls* COLETTE *onto the bed and kisses her. A* Châtelaine *magazine lolls from her hand. Its cover girl: Michaëlle Jean.*]

M: You're sleek and stylish—like *Flare* magazine:
A bodacious stunner, a Suzanne Boyd gamine.

C: To be a mandarin, I dress like mannequins—
Silhouettes modelled on adolescent women.

M: If you can't be good, then look good: that's my style.
Moral codes mimic dress codes—what's in fashion.

C: Everyone in Québec struts a style—
it's our definitive definition.

M: That's why Montreal makes Toronto
look as dreary as Edmonton.

C: When first to Québec I came,
I stood once in this endless forest
With endless snow tumbling around—
Snow, snow, snow, tumbling around,
I trembled so in that frosty forest,
When first to Québec I came.

M: I remember fields snowy with clover
fronting that feral Nova Scotian Ocean,
its blue-grey circumflexes of waves,
and I see my mother's gold-leaf face,
gleaming, as my rum-coloured father,
brought me a toy piano, black and silver,
echoing a classic *Bösendorfer.*

C: *On peut toujours jaser....*

M: *On peut encore s'embrasser.*

C: *Je t'aimmmmmmme*, Malcolm.

M: I love you, too, Colette, my balm.

C: *Je t'aime beaucoup, beaucoup. À ce soir.*

M: *Oui, à ce soir,*
that hour just before
indigo melts azure to *noir*.

[COLETTE *jumps up, kisses* MALCOLM, *and leaves.*]

Scene ii: Récit d'Ovide

[*Wearing a black beret, a black Nehru jacket, and black pants,* MALCOLM *stands at the bar of La Révolution Tranquille. He flutes lime-coloured absinthe into a glass. Dressed in a white jacket, red pants, and mauve shirt,* OVIDE *downs it. His gold crucifix glints. A vase fountains sunflowers.*]

O: Absinthe maketh the heart grow fonder, eh?

M: If not that, it cuts it asunder.

[MALCOLM *drinks.* OVIDE *looks out the window. He wolf-whistles. He aims his video camera at the window.*]

O: Is it their nylons, that sheer, shimmering
Polyhexamethyleneudiapide, simmering,
That sets girls' legs chicly glimmering?

M: Uh huh, Québec Cité's *panochitas*
Say "*Buona notte*" with *aqua vitae*.

What man doesn't want some of that—
Some adorably filthy *fille-appât*?

O: I adore cosmo mosaics—rainbows—of women:
Their peach-copper hair, their plum-cocoa skin,
Their almond-amber eyes that are an eyeful,
Their beauty surpassing everything beautiful.

Sometimes I spend whole nights just imagining—
Kissing, tonguing, drooling, slurping, sinning.

M: This mania you mention, so manic and mad,
Screens like a scene scripted by Sade....

O: [*Singing.*] "Love your wife, tooth and nail:
Moulder in the *Marriage* jail.
Love your whore, fang and claw:
Make *Adultery* the law."

M: Now, you echo consciously surly, early Pound
Reading late, great Yeats where the dreaming Shelley drowned.

O: There was a woman. *Il y avait une femme*.
Her cigarette smoke spangled, silvery, posh—
Haloing *une nouvelle* Coco Chanel.... Gosh!

There was a woman. *Il y avait une femme*—
All silky black blouses and carousing curls
And inky black skirts, milky, slinky pearls.

So Dante-elegant, débutante-delicate....

M: To use the blackest Black English I know, "No shit?!!"

O: How hot it was, that summer, didn't matter:
Her hot, scalding kisses burned even hotter.

I sing of a white woman who was whitest white—
Like smoke or fog or mist.

[OVIDE *turns and addresses the sunflowers. He sets down his camera, picks up a flower, and holds it before him like a microphone.*]

O: Sunflowers, in your aureate, snowing light—
Half-gold, half-amethyst—
Sunflowers, in your aureate, snowing light,
We kissed and kissed and kissed.

M: A pallid gal crowning a black man's sex:
She was Desdemona, you was Oedipus Rex.

O: I say nothing reticent and nothing rhetorical:
All her beauty was pretty allegorical.

She was cute, homespun *haute couture*—
Glamourous, amorous, *une belle du jour*.

M: Or molten, sparkling, ivory gloss—
La dolce vita, la vie en rose?

O: There was a woman. *Il y avait une femme*.
Even weather was not as hot as she! Damn!

Our dalliance, *mésalliance*, had a blues blueprint:
We founded love that crumbled like poor cement.

M: The girl was a ruin. You left her crying?

O: Mireille was dismaying and dissatisfying.

M: But Laxmi?

O: A *femme fatale* Salomé, pure silk and teak,
Her carriage Georgian, her columns Greek.

The curvature of space?
Who cares?
Her curves erase
All fears.

The beauty of Time?
So what?
Her thinness is what Time
Has not....

But she seems indifferent—
In different ways,
Suspicious of kisses
And cold to clichés.

Though very exotic, sensual, feminine,
Very shapely, very sexy, so ultra-clean—

Lush in skirts, lush in heels, lush in everything–
She isn't open-minded: she's no libertine....

M: You sound like you're teetering at a cliff.

O: I could find Love, a way to be loved, if....

M: [*Shrugging.*] Those who can, can-can.
Those who can't, go to Cannes
And seduce disingenuous, sinuous *ingénues*.

O: Oh, what's the use? Oh, what's the use?

Seductions, in sum, succumb to the sordid—
Then gell to amours, mortifying and morbid.

[MALCOLM *puts away the absinthe.* OVIDE *goes absent.*]

Scene iii: Sur le pont

– On the bridge

[*On Le Pont de Québec, a cantilever bridge,* OVIDE *stands at the pedestrian railing. In the sheer night, le fleuve Saint-Laurent seems like smoked chrome. Tipsily,* OVIDE *pulls a photograph from his jacket pocket.*]

O: See April water swarming in channels
Indigo under dark-blue atmospheres;

See white foam churning black, abysmal,
In cataracts as cataclysmic as tears.

This annihilating nadir I see
Is eel-black, eel-slick, eel-slippery.

[OVIDE *pitches the photograph into the wind, into airy, then liquid, pitch.*]

O: Our essence is need:
To be born is to crave—
To gasp for air,
To grasp for Love.

Farewell, Mireille. *Oui, adieu*.
Only the sky should be blue.

[OVIDE *begins to leave the bridge. The chasm beneath is a canyon.*]

A whirlwind

Scene iv: Au funiculaire

[OVIDE *(in blue pants, a lime-green jacket, yellow shirt, and black shoes) and* LAXMI *(in a gold necklace with pink sapphires, a black suede skirt, pale-green turtleneck and cardigan, and black pumps) stand on la terrasse Dufferin in front of le funiculaire, the building housing the hill-climbing elevator that shuttles voyageurs between La Haute-Ville and La Basse-Ville. Sound of whirring as the glass-sheathed funiculaire itself arrives at its station in the lit-up building. There is moonlight without and Le Château Frontenac is in the background.*]

L: A single star weds
the space between two branches.
My eyes bear witness.

O: The moon expands its white domains, intakes
Territory upon territory,
Increases its white hold on seas, shadows, stars,
And drives night into silvery exile.
My heart is a like imperialist—
Annexing states outside itself....

L: Why ogle voluptuously the moon—or stars? *Je m'en fous.*
Scrutinize the scarily cascading *l'escalier Casse-Cou.*

O: To cap a night of sushi and tiramisù,
Cue the boudoir ballads of Sade Adu.
Laissez-vous séduire....

L: No, Ovide, *je vais prendre le funiculaire*
À La Basse-Ville,
Et puis le traversier home to Lévis.

O: Your face is this night, brimming ivory stars:
Quelle beauté!
Your skin's smooth—like paper without writing:
Quelle poésie!

L: Your metaphors, *monsieur*, are pure European.

O: Laxmi, I'm 100 per cent, humanist Aquarian!

I know who I am: son of Montreal—
Metropolis *noir*, a black capital—
With Nelson Symonds on guitar, Oliver Jones on piano:
Where being bilingual is being biracial and bisexual too.

L: Marie-Josèphe Angélique
is my Québécoise idol:
that abused slave, proud, *tragique*,
incinerated Montréal....

O: History is old; that's why it's history.
Voyons the wet, glistening geography
De la Chute de Montmorency.

L: *Je me souviens*, Québec's motto, says it all:
We are the heirs of History's crushing pall.

Apply a plain philosophy of light:
History looms in the future, darkly.

O: To recover, discover Anurima Banerji:
Her lyricism legitimates intimacy.

L: To understand me, read Lorena Gale—
Une Québécoise—Afro-Asian-Aboriginal.

Or try Mitiarjuk Nappaluk or Ying Chen
Or Nigel Thomas or Gérard Étienne.

But "Real Spittoonbath," I deplore:
Yeshim Ternar is superbly superior.

[LAXMI *turns from* OVIDE *and enters the 'cable car.'* OVIDE *places his right palm against its window.*]

O: Laxmi, my love's as long as the Saint Lawrence River!—
My simple, simple, unpretending love.... O lover!

(Must I make song after song, but not make love?
Must all my love songs be sung for others?)

[LAXMI *places her left palm against the inside window as le funiculaire descends, slant-wise, away from* OVIDE.]

L: Every evening can't end in epicurean epiphanies—
Nor with *Laura Secord* truffles after *Breakfast at Tiffany's*.

Ovide, I'm no "Sanskrit, Allophone enigma,"
Nor some "coconut-jasmine-rosewater replica"....

Love isn't just the functional
Conjunctions of curves angular—
Or painless screwings that resemble
Assembling Swedish furniture.

No more aggressive kisses
Striking at me like cobras!

No more smutty Sutras!
          No more Romance mantras!

The heart is suspect architecture:
It must be transparent steel, not lead veneer.

[*Le funiculaire stops at its lower 'station' and* LAXMI *departs from it and the building. A svelte, sultry odalisque, her movements mark a renaissance of flavour.*]

Scene v: Au magasin de confection

[*In a dress shop tattooed with a sign promising, "La Nouvelle Vague,"* COLETTE, *in a Nova Scotian tartan sari, examines a rack of gem-coloured blouses.* LAXMI *enters. She wears a blazing pink sarong—and a turquoise necklace—and white pumps.*]

L: Ah, Colette! Is this boutique where you work?

C: No. In the firm Layton Cohen, I'm a clerk.

L: I'm at Hydro-Québec—as an assistant
          to a Chief Deputy, Deputy Assistant.

I see saris are in vogue, and you're in love.
Am I right? I am right. Rightly, I approve.

C: Laxmi Bharati, I do admit I adore
The blue-black tinting his skin and hair;
That black indigo in Malcolm's hair….
Blackness blacker than black, I adore.

L: Beware: Men have sex, but women have babies.
Men 'make love', but women make 'mistakes.'

Why must we be comic *Hymenoptera*,
our mandibles and incisors and feelers
clutching and biting and gnawing
in sex acts that dissect insect opera?

C: All women should, I'm sure you'll approve,
Give love and have love and make love.

L: To be sexually dirty, but still seem wholesome:
Is what primes cosmetics and Romanticism.

Men's desire is to deflower,
        devour, and depart.
They annex your sex
        and, after, snort, and ask, "Who's next?"

C: Men's morals are desolate, detritus.
But must women be acidic or citrus?

L: The impermanence of flowers
Souls do not have.
Thus, Love for aeons, not hours,

We rightly crave.
Spirit's what weds us: flesh sours,
Sinks, to the grave.

C: Malcolm and I are of linked vision,
But united by no mere thing.
Coupled with passionate precision,
We form a single chain of Being.

The essence of our twinned *québécité*
Is an indelibly doubled haecceity.

What about you and your avid Ovide?

L: I'm myself, pure, still, and he is—still—Ovide....

Have you told your parents about Malcolm?

C: [*Wildly.*] I can't! I can't! I can't bring him home!

L: So you see him secretly, sneak out and back?
Because he's black. Right? Because he's black.

C: How cold you are! A cold virago with cold eyes,
A cold heart, cold words, ice-cold philosophies.

L: But I'm no hypocrite, no polished ascetic
With gilded morals, but rusty *practique*.

If you're so lyrically in love, Legal Aid girl,
Brave your parents; face, anew, this backward world.

[*This leaf—or page—crackles, "Leave!"* LAXMI *leaves.* COLETTE *weeps.*]

C: Everything about our pairing is despairing.
Despair is everything about our pairing.

All our Reality is shades of wars:
First, yellow sunlight blacks out the stars,
Then the sun crashes into crimson seas
And bursts into stars—black, burning stars.

Scene vi: Devant l'Hôtel du Parlement

[*Before le Palais législatif, that silver-grey, rococo edifice (Law and Architecture married),* LAXMI, *in a beige jacket, white camisole, beige skirt, white nylons, and glossy caramel pumps, strolls with* OVIDE. *He wears a black jacket, blue shirt, and cream pants. Pastel tulips tint the monochromatic legislature.*]

O: Over there, across the valley, beyond Sillery,
Pines sprout, dark as rains, but silvery.

L: Black pines gather: like crowds of mourners
Around Love, that diseased body, coronary....

O: Love is human: even some chilly aristocrat
Warms to a slut, hot from the proletariat.

L: Impure houri, of impudent pudenda,
Imprudently satisfy hetaerae agenda.

O: Why such pretty—I mean—petrifying words?
The city glistens with wedding-cake light!

L: Often Marriage
ends as mirage—
or in *triage*—
or in a cage.

O: Laxmi, in Delibes's apt opera, *Lakmé*,
The Hindu Juliet enacts Love's acme.

I don't ask for half as much, nor vaunt
Queries to irk, irritate, and itch.

L: I'll ask one: "What does a woman want?"
The answer's "To be young, single, and rich."

O: Must we spat outside Québec's parliament?
*Ici nous sommes—tous—*Québécois, *suprêmement*.

L: "*La peau brune, mais le coeur québécois*"?
Tell that to the "*pure laine*" Québécois!

Everybody here asks me if I'm Indienne,
If I answer "Canadian," they ask, "Since when?"

When Parizeau, paranoid, blamed "*le vote ethnique*"
For his Referendum loss, his disgust was chic.
I knew then that all Québécois must be white
Or could not be Québécois, at least not quite.

I'll never be Québécoise *de souche*, *un pepsi*:
I'm Indian, indubitably, nixing nympholepsy.

Why show solicitude for folks' *québécitude*
When nativists negate, denigrate, *négritude*?

Why not trumpet Quebec's aboriginal origin,
Its very name that is Abenaki—Algonquin?

Neither be a *péquiste* nor a *libéral*.

O: The only thing you must feel is, is—beautiful!

But admit Canada's a tolerably "tolerant" space....

L: What about Anthony Griffin? Or the Van de Peere case—
When the Supreme Court alleged, "*We* don't see race"—
Then whited out Blacks, Black cultures effaced?

O: When my parents left Haiti, dodging Duvalier,
Le Parti Québécois said, "*Venez, restez.*"

L: My Brahmin parents flew from Mumbai—
A doctor and a teacher, once of Bombay.
They arc'd that sea, that cerulean sea,

To foster fortunes and a future for me.
Now, I'll copper temples and tile cathedrals—
To satisfy, harmonize, spiritual souls.

O: If you were to die right now, you'd regret,
Not having loved, not having been fit.

L: Why would I regret not being lied to?

[OVIDE *strides away.* LAXMI *chases after him and grabs his arm.* OVIDE *turns, pulls* LAXMI *roughly to him. He kisses her. She slaps him.*]

O: Now I regret.... I love you.

L: How can three words stand for as much as that?
It's just Tin Pan Alley-glitzy, chintzy chit-chat!

O: Your virtue is just as clichéd as Bollywood—
An antique in real life, a boutique in Hollywood!

L: Men's sex is outer, all women's inner:
Upon each lies each shameless sinner.

O: It's surrealism more unreal than a Dali—
All your inimical cynicism about sex!

L: Beware: my household goddess is seven-armed Kali,
Who swings seven swords and severs seven necks!

[OVIDE *exits, furiously.*]

Scene vii: À l'extérieur de la boîte de nuit

[*In a dark dusk, glowering outside La Révolution Tranquille,* MALCOLM, *in beige pants and shirt, and a brown-pinstripe beige jacket with matching tie, plus white Panama hat and tan suede shoes, faces a tearful* COLETTE. *She wears a black ballerina tulle skirt, an ivory petticoat with black lace frills at cuffs and collar, and three-strap black shoes. The mood is Dior—and dire.*]

M: So your parents denounce me as a "nigger"?
Now, ain't that some shit? Sugar!

C: That's not what they meant.
That's not what they mean.

M: I know what they mean—
"a brutal physiognomy,
ignoble, igneous ignominy."
Oh, I know what they mean!

Québécois claim they're "white niggers of America,"
Peut-être, but I'm the Negro *nègre* of Québec!
Merde! Merde! Archetypal *merde!*
Franchement! Nous sommes absurdes! Absurdes!

C: We can still love. Don't be so mean!

M: I want to love meaningfully,
not meanly.

You can't force a song.
You can't force a duet.
It mustn't feel wrong—
Lest it's illicit.

C: I thought I was hallucinating
when Mama swore she'd suicide.
She stuck a steak knife at her heart,
but she was really aiming it at my heart,
and I felt it go in.
Next, Papa grabbed her wrist,
arrested the blade,
but told me I am banished.
I saw my parents holding knives,
shouting down Love,
yelling blasphemies at each other.
I stumbled, dizzy, out these doors,
tears replacing my eyes.

M: Loving you is like, like, Heaven and a lynching!
Pops abandoned Tennessee to flee such flinching!
For lavish Love, motorcycled to Nova Scotia,
Affianced, married, an Afro-Mi'kmaq madonna.

C: Must I just destroy my parents' hearts?
They dream of golden, Chinese grandchildren.
Can I coldly stab their dreaming hearts?

M: It's theirs—or mine—or ours.

Are Chinese *pure laine* like some Québécois?
Am I a black sheep, a devil, dizzyingly *noir*?

C: Would our children be black or gold?
Would they be free or free to be sold?

M: Do you think our kids'd be striped like zebras?
Or look like Neapolitan ice cream? Or amoebas?

C: Will you obnubilate
our Beauty?
Will you repudiate
my duty?

[*Crying.*] My folks said you can't perform here,
If you don't forget and forsake me.

M: Well, hell, no, my quartet won't play!
We'll put our silver instruments
And our sable music away. Away!
This ain't no time for Innocence.

Away! Away! Away! Away! Away!

[MALCOLM *walks into the nightclub, rips down his band's poster, and storms out and away.*]

Canto III

The production IS the beloved.

POUND, CANTO CIV

Malcolm outside of the hotel.

Scene i: Malcolm à l'extérieur de l'hôtel

[MALCOLM *paces before Le Château Frontenac. He wears a paper-white shirt, a pinkish cream suit, a scarlet tie, and dark sunglasses. His suitcase and instrument case occupy a hotel luggage cart. Night!* MALCOLM *unlocks his horn case. He holds up his saxophone. The night gleams mournfully.*]

M: Oh Colette,
I can't forget.

I cry
the smell of goodbye
in the way you vanished,
ma jolie Chinoise-Québécoise,
folding yourself away
like a map
of ghostly geography.

I cry
the absence of our whole
Québec Crisis of French
tongue, sweet grammar
of our thighs,
conjugating all night.

I cry
because you're gone,
gone though Parliament
pleaded with you to stay.

I cry
the oval, open mouth
of your goodbye.

[*Crying,* MALCOLM *removes his sunglasses, wipes his eyes, then packs up his saxophone. It is like the night is being put away.*]

M: I'll not be a decomposing composer,
Asphyxiating his gasping sax.
God, damn a keep-quiet revolution!
I'll holler Love maximally max!

[MALCOLM *beckons for a taxi. Black birds feast—*
and coast—on light.]

M: I am a star; Colette's a galaxy.
Taxi! Taxi! My music for a taxi!

Scene ii: Colette au bar

[*Inside the dark La Révolution Tranquille,* COLETTE, *in a white dress patterned with black bars of music, sits at the bar. She opens a bottle of absinthe and pours the smoking verdancy into a martini glass. She daubs at her eyes. She tosses aside her cellphone. Her tea-black hair is raining, sweetly.*]

C: Finally, I'm *called* to the bar—
the bar of prosecution,

the bar of ripped-up bars of Music,
the bar of persecution,
and the bar of inebriation,
and the bar of intoxication....

Africa is far from China, yes,
    but their histories harmonize:
On its "yellow niggers,"
    Canada a head tax incised,
but bid my slaving ancestors
    lay down its rail ties;
their blood scoured the iron road
    flashing Gold Mountain's skies.

But China's not Shangri-la or Eden:
    Mao declared jazz seditious contraband.
He branded its sound "bourgeois decadent,"
    Then quickly commanded that it be banned.

Yes, jazz is a black-market, black-magic Music:
Its Voodoo fuses Malcolm X and Confucius.

Now I lust for the look of leaves, leaves in fresh wind,
Blown startlingly green against Malcolm's sable skin!

Why can't we have May rains in April?
Why can't Joy flower just like maples?

Oh, why can't we have darling rain
    curling over our faces in cafés again?

Malcolm, when I'm below and you're above,
Our Yin-Yang will make common sense of Love.

I'll drink deep your kisses—
 right to the back of my mouth.

Scene iii: Ovide sur le pont

[*While winds buffet his black cape,* OVIDE, *dressed in a scarlet shirt and black suit (Stendhal colours), stands again upon Le Pont de Québec.* OVIDE *stares into the distant void of le fleuve Saint-Laurent—a flash flood of indifference.*]

O: My heart, still beating, syncopates Tragedy.
I've exchanged bliss for some blues obscenity.

Like a pen-and-ink poet, destitute of song,
I've served perverse verse: concrete,
 L=A=N=G=U=A=G=E, sprung. [*lah-nggwij*]

A sole, sullen love can solo far too far—
Like light driving to us from a cold, dead star.

O! Her beauty could topple Plato
And give eyeless statues eyes too.

[OVIDE *climbs over the bridge railing and prepares to jump.*]

O: Before her eyes, I, a poem, changed to fire,
And she backed away.
Now her looks suffocate me, like this wind.
I am moral decay.

A thousand voices say I lie to say
I love, and charge me
With inconstancy. How can I naysay?
I've lived *louche* lechery.

Laxmi's virtues poets hardly imagine—
Even in a Senghorian alexandrine.

My heart seethes as furiously as the river:
But what if—Laxmi, her love, I recover?

Scene iv: Laxmi sur le quai

[*In the fog-white night,* LAXMI, *sporting a long black suede overcoat, an orange silk scarf, black leather boots, and a violet and gold mid-length dress, walks along the ferry terminal dock. She is a* diva devi—*de souche. A sign indicates Le Traversier for Lévis. Sound of a foghorn. This music is no discrepancy.*]

L: This foggy, tubercular chill makes April hurt!
When will the ferry deliver me from such murk?

This water, oil-dark, is conspicuously viscous:
It surges, shines, as promiscuous as hibiscus.

I try to see Reality uncut, uncensored:
Ovide is a parade of prettied-up dirt.

He painted me as "*une pute exotique—*
une lascivité proprement asiatique."

Mais, je ne suis pas une débutante lubrique,
avec "une chatte gluante, pimentée, impudique."

No, a true love must prove honourable and pure.
My husband must also be our children's father.

He who'd love me—inviolate—must love
Eros immaculate, *His* aureate trove.

Scene v: Dans le brouillard

[COLETTE *(in an ivory ermine cape fringed with a sable collar)* *and* OVIDE *wander separately in fog. Their songs interlock.*]

C: This seascape is purloined from Li Po—
Just mist, mist, and water everywhere....
But where is Malcolm, where are his eyes?

O: This sky coffining us, oh, I deserve!
Clouds are sinking down in mire.
My heart's a dire abyss of bias.

C: I should go naked in the fur of snow,
Sprawl in its soft chill and weight,
Feel raw cold corset my breasts, my thighs.

O: Laxmi mirrors *belle époque* India,
Exquisite, sepia-toned, lavish, precise.
But I've spouted fog—opaque, white lies.

[*Into the scene drifts* LAXMI, *followed distantly by* MALCOLM, *so that all four players are mutually lost in the fog, each oblivious to the others.*]

L: Ovide, I lust for Love, a love I can lionize—
A man so good he makes good memories.

M: Oh Colette, you are Love in disguise—
I'll confess, I regret, I'll apologize.

O: Laxmi's a Chola bronze, lavish, precise.

C: But where is Malcolm, where are his eyes?

C&O: Malcolm, Laxmi, do not let our romance end:
I miss you as hurtingly as a kite misses wind.

L&M: Like a kite misses wind.

[*The wanderers continue off on their separate searches.*]

Scene vi: Sur le quai

[*In a taxi,* MALCOLM *arrives at the ferry terminal. He sees* LAXMI, *pacing. He steps out and removes his suitcase and his saxophone case. Then* MALCOLM *approaches* LAXMI.]

L: Malcolm, aren't you playing tonight?
Why divagate in this cold, dull light?

M: Colette's parents have parted me from their daughter,
But I'll seek her, Laxmi, across this parting water.

Night is wet and cold with unweatherable sorrow.
What, after immeasurable Pleasure, but Sorrow?

L: I'm sorry for this news about your love.

M: What of Ovide and your Sacré Coeur of love?

[LAXMI *begins to weep silently.*]

L: My *châteaux* are ruins of Romance—
and your rupture with Colette
is my fault. I nagged Colette
to tell her folks your romance.

M: Soon or late, they'd know, I knew, about us.

L: And Ovide was pushy, pushy like Priapus.

[MALCOLM *opens his suitcase and offers his bottle of absinthe to* LAXMI.]

L: I really shouldn't; perhaps it's impure.

M: Sorrow improves with a good liqueur.

[LAXMI *accepts the phallic bottle, tips it carefully, and sips.*]

M: So Ovide's a *papier-mâché* playboy, *un poseur,*
A masher, *pas un gentilhomme de couleur*?

L: Oh, why must men be born immoral?

M: True: our high notes are only musical....
But Ovide's no more egotistical
Than any man-child who boasts testicles.

L: Rapacity is the only male capacity,
Violating Virtue in every vicinity.

M: I know Ovide's an unstable Lothario.

L: He's more a Ripper-type than a Romeo.

M: Ovide is Prufrockian, defrocked, fucked up.
But, Laxmi, you need Humility to love.

L: I don't need any man. What's matrimony?
C'est un bordel dans une chienlit.

M: Happiness takes work; Pleasure is exacting.
Joy requires exercise; it's not play-acting.

L: Marriage can't be left to mere amateurs:
Amours must be lived as a *tour de force*.

M: You detest Vice, but Ovide's not so vicious:
Why deem Desire despicable malpractice?

L: I keep the Wisdom of my Mama:
Trust the faithful God of Death, Yama,
Next, the God of Chastity, Rama,
But, dead last, the God of Love, Kama.

M: Is that any reason, Laxmi, for this drama?

L: When I was twelve, I accidentally saw
Father kissing some shocking Québécoise:
She was viscous, a creamy *vichyssoise*.
He didn't know I saw, clear viciousness saw.

M: Put aside your father's betrayal,
Laxmi, if you love Ovide at all.

L: I love Ovide because I shouldn't
(because he so enrages me,
because he does so outrageously,
things I wouldn't or couldn't)....

Your advice, Malcolm, should you abet.
So how now will you recollect Colette?

M: She tried to reason with me; Love was Reason.
But, oh, I've committed reckless treason.

[MALCOLM *takes the absinthe, drinks, and weeps.*]

L: It's not too late. Confront her parents.

M: I hadn't thought I should, but now I must.

L: A woman has only her trust in trust.
Men have their calculated indifference.

[*The night fog is punctured by footsteps.* COLETTE *appears.* LAXMI *fades into shadows.*]

C: Malcolm, I searched everywhere! Please come home,
To whatever home we both can found *ensemble*.

[MALCOLM *and* COLETTE *embrace and kiss. A foghorn sounds.*]

M: I must go and face—face down—your parents.

C: To cleave as one, we don't need their clearance.

You and I have been through much—
And should not surrender touch.

M: In this rain mumblin, bumblin, round,
In this rain grumblin, rumblin, round,
Without you, I got no solid ground.

C: Africans and Chinese jointly adore
Musicals, spices, teas, watercolours.
We are too alike not, too, to be *ours*.

M: Let's start our own *révolution tranquille*,
with a wrecking ruckus, gay with glee—
an unquiet riot—
half in bed and half out.

[MALCOLM *and* COLETTE *kiss. Then* MALCOLM *takes up his saxophone and descants scattered, melodic scales.* LAXMI *coughs to announce her presence. She emerges, gleaming, from the shadows.*]

C: [*To* LAXMI.] You are unpleasant, plus unwanted.

M: Truth may be unpleasant, but is always wanted.

L: Hear: I recant, Colette, the doubts I decanted.

M: [*To* COLETTE.] Laxmi and I were mourning you and Ovide.

C: Let us resolve: Love must be plucked from the void.

[*A foghorn sounds. The Lévis ferry arrives.*]

L: *Voici le traversier*. I'll say "*Bonsoir*," Malcolm, Colette.

C: Laxmi, stay with us awhile, stay awhile yet.

[*Through the mist, haggard, the black-caped* OVIDE *appears.* LAXMI *and* OVIDE *eye each other, pause, then close, embrace, and kiss.*]

O: I heard Malcolm's saxophone from the boat.
It was Karma to follow—like Fate—each note.

[MALCOLM *and* COLETTE *approach the other pair.*]

M&C: Believers, lovers,
you must begin again.

O: [*To* LAXMI.] Your eyes are luculent obsidian.

Cut me and gold will flow out—
that's Love when mixed with air.

C: The stars, swinging, swinging, in their course,
Want everyone to have everything, *sans* divorce.

L: Ovide, I'll bring you Enlightenment yet.
You'll be my *Kabir*, my *ghazal*-poet.

O: I'll compose a whole opera on Love.

L: Please omit jealousy, deceit, and hate.

M: This time, Colette, perfected I will prove.

C: Let's waltz in styles cinematic, up-to-date.

L: We'll love without skill, but without scheming.

M: Oh, if I were King of Nouvelle-Écosse….

C: (You know you break no laws by dreaming!)

M: Love would be *bel*, not bellicose.

[*The two couples ballet a contemporary, Québec quadrille.*
Oriental-occidental, instrumental music appears.
The ferry moans.]

O: Laxmi, I'm prodigal, my mouth full of songs;
My eyes seek lush light; rum honeys my lungs.
I like baroque structures, those bashfully soft.
Please, *acushla*, accept this luscious gift.

[OVIDE *withdraws a roll of papers from his inner coat pocket.*]

O: *Voici* blueprints for a stained-glass cathedral—
To celebrate Laxmi, Kali, *et avril*.

[LAXMI *embraces* OVIDE. *They kiss.* COLETTE *and* MALCOLM *applaud.*]

L: I'd like a temple, *mera pyar*, not a cathedral….
But I'll help you erect it, for I'm your equal.
Our motto will be *Satyam, Shivam, Sundarum*—

Or *Truth, God, Beauty*—three words that rhyme.

[MALCOLM *removes a small box from his coat pocket. He kneels.*]

M: [*To* COLETTE.] I will still ask your parents for your hand,
But it's handsome I ask *you* for your hand.

[MALCOLM *opens the box to free a cocoa diamond ring.*
As MALCOLM *slides it onto* COLETTE'S *finger, she kisses him.*
LAXMI *and* OVIDE *applaud.*]

M: I propose we marry on May the First.
Those who oppose Love be fools God-cursed.

C: I love you! O! The delicious jazz we'll make!

L&O: Put away tears; *au revoir*, heartbreak.

[COLETTE *reaches into her pocket and hands* MALCOLM
a clementine.]

M: Mine clement, clement clementine.

C: Let's love until air turns to banked flame
And seas boil away into the stars.

O: [*To* LAXMI.] We'll be oral linguists tonguing French vocables.

L: Let your lips crush mine with sincerity.

[*The couples kiss.*]

O: Love is as giving as a spoon,
Endures as stainless as the moon,
Keeps freshly fertile—just like June.

L: Love is air that all things must have.
Without Love, it is impossible to live.

M: Each seed digs a grave; still, Love's ever-fresh:
We'll dance our marriage in the bonds of flesh.

C: I always want to meet you, golden in the dawn,
With nothing, blessèd nothing, but just our smiles on.

Scene vii: Le finale

[*Under a banner proclaiming, "1 mai, Fête des travailleurs, Fête du printemps,"* COLETTE, *wearing a white-lace Mao suit, plus a white diaphanous veil, and carrying red roses and a white-lace parasol, stands with the black-tuxed* MALCOLM. *They are joined by the sable-tuxed* OVIDE *and by* LAXMI, *who is dressed in a Zuhair Murad-designed, scarlet-and-gold sari, drenched in gold jewellery, and carrying white lotus. Her hands are embroidered with henna. The couples stand before the gleaming Le Château Frontenac.* OVIDE *films everyone with his video camera and then sets it aside. (This scene recalls May 68: Trudeaumania in Canada, Pre-Raphaelite Marxism in Czechoslovakia, and classy, sexy revolt in France.)*]

M&O: She is sea-smoked beach.
I am the province's poem.
She is wild apple, russet.
I am dark and pungent rum.

C&L: Apple blossoms, rain-wet,
Froth and foam in our groves.
Our *rati* begins in speech:
April sounds perennial loves.

ALL: May ushers in with lilac—
sweet apple blossoms too—
cutting in buttery,
fluttering,
suave colours of cream plum
and honey *pluviôse*
plus perfumes fuming
musky lemon,
and smells of cedar in fresh rain.

We are not only
        philosophies and religions,
languages and 'races,'
        but also skin and breath,
thought and blood,
        and on that basis,

that axis,
        yes, *oui*, may amalgamate
and mate and propagate
        just as we wish.

Our children will be
        every colour eyes can know,
and free:
        and states, parents, gods,
must have no say:
        Love is a tyrannical democracy.

Vive le Québec.
Vive le Québec.
Vive le Québec libéré.

Vive aussi le Québec de couleur—
Toutes les couleurs.
Vive notre québécité.

[*The lovers exit as couples—riding Vespa scooters. Then church bells, horns, sitar, Chinese violin (p'i-p'a), harmonium, harp, tabla, and thumb piano commix. The Québec flag descends from the rafters, but its four panels are, here, beige, pink, gold, and indigo, and its fleurs-de-lys are, correspondingly, violet, orange, black, and crimson, and its cruciform segmentation is green.*]

— *Fin* —

Miscellaneous Explications

p. 24 "Imitate Holland-Dozier-Holland ❡ Eddy and Brian Holland and Lamont Dozier, Motown songwriters.

p. 25 "As Laferrière's in *How to Make Love to a Negro*" ❡ Dany Laferrière, *Comment faire l'amour avec un negre sans se fatiguer*, 1985. Traslation by David Homel, *How to Make Love to a Negro*, 1987.

p. 26 "I like the legalese, neo-Chinese, of Pierre Trudeau" ❡ Jacques Hébert et Pierre Elliott Trudeau, *Deux Innocents en Chine rouge*, 1961.

p. 36 "No, it's more like, *oui*, J.J. Jackson, / His 1966 hit, 'But It's Alright'" ❡ Jackson & Tubbs, "But It's Alright," 1966.

p. 66 "*La peau brune, mais le coeur québécois*" ❡ Québec government pro-sovereignty advertisement, Summer 1995.

p.67 "When Parizeau, paranoid, blamed '*le vote ethnique*'" ❡ Québec Premier Jacques Parizeau, October 30, 1995.

p. 67 "What about Anthony Griffin? Or the Van de Peere case…?" ❡ Griffin was an unarmed black youth shot dead by a white Montreal policeman after being arrested for non-payment of a taxi fare in Fall 1987; Kimberley Van de Peere v. Theodore Edwards and Valerie Cooper Edwards, Supreme Court of Canada Judgement, in a black-and-white, biracial child custody case, September 28, 2001.

p. 69 "Québécois claim they're 'white niggers of America'" ❡ Pierre Vallières, *Nègres blancs d'Amérique*, 1968. Translation by Joan Pinkham, *White Niggers of America*, 1971.

"You know you break no laws by dreaming": George Elliott Clarke's Québécité

A POSTLUDE BY AJAY HEBLE

Jazz opera: not a well-documented genre, to be sure, but *that*, I suspect, may well be part of its allure. Alert with the snap of the new and untried, and unfettered by settled habits of convention, this hybrid genre compels us to imagine an alternative vision of human possibility. It's a grand objective, I admit, but let's recall that opera has almost always been about grand-scale gestures, about excess, about staging the spectacular. Throw jazz into the mix, and what you get, as George Elliott Clarke's libretto for *Québécité* so eloquently, so resiliently, demonstrates, is a gumbo concoction: one where hope and imagination rainbow over orthodoxy, where the capacity to dream reinvigorates our commitment to new understandings of identity, belonging, and collective social responsibility.

The libretto's title, *Québécité*, is itself deliberately and playfully provocative, especially considering the mixed-race couples at the centre of the plot, and in light, too, of the fraught role that ethnicity and race have played in struggles for Québec nationalism. Eschewing the exclusivist, monolithic, and anti-ethnic sentiments that too often attach themselves to expressions of national or cultural identity—think, for example, of Jacques Parizeau's now infamous remarks in October 1995 about how the "ethnic vote" defeated his attempts to win sovereignty for Québec—Clarke's emphasis on "*le Québec de couleur*" represents a bold attempt to counter the demonization of the "other" in attempts to fashion homogeneous national communities. Indeed, as cultural theorist George Lipsitz writes, "During times of economic decline and social disintegration, it is tempting for people to blame their problems on others, and to seek succor and certainty from racist and nationalist myths. But the desire to seek certainty and stability by depicting the world solely as one story told from one point of view," Lipsitz argues, "is more dangerous than ever before" (132). With *Québécité*, George Elliott Clarke seeks to break free from these monolithic ways of knowing the world, and instead engages in an explicit broadening of the cultural scope of (and subject matter for) new Canadian opera.

Clarke's efforts to work towards a more inclusive understanding of issues such as belonging, identity, and citizenship is, moreover, worth thinking about in relation to comments he himself has made on the Canada-Québec schism. In the introduction to his 1997 anthology of African Canadian writing, *Eyeing the North Star: Directions in African Canadian Literature*, a text whose own *raison d'être* Clarke explicitly articulates in terms of an insistence on "new, more inclusive definitions of Canadianness" (xxiii), he writes, "The primacy assigned the Canada-Québec schism marginalizes all other ethnic-racial-linguistic questions" (xvii). In this context, Clarke "references the pandemonium that then-Parti Québecois MNA Jean Alfred, a Haitian Canadian, aroused at a National Black Coalition of Canada meeting in Toronto in May 1979, when he declared, before a hundred delegates at the King Edward Hotel, that Québec's 'liberation' was more important than black national unity" (xvii). Clarke's point in recalling this episode is that "language dynamics drive some black francophone intellectuals to prioritize linguistic issues ahead of racial matters" (xvii). Now *Québécité*, clearly, isn't making a statement about black national unity, and it isn't—as anyone who reckons with the richness, the playfulness, and the extraordinary musicality of Clarke's poetry will immediately recognize—about to pay short shrift to the vitality of language; it does, however, exert a necessary challenge to mainstream assumptions about Québec as white. And in this context, its non-compliance with dominant knowledge-producing elites in Canada seems to me to carry a salutary—indeed an urgent—political force.

That force is perhaps most profoundly registered in the text's insistence on the power to dream. "You know you break no laws by dreaming," announces one of the opera's characters, Colette Chan, as the libretto draws us towards its finale. Colette's remark hastens us to reflect on the fact that the capacity to dream (as Martin Luther King's famous "I have a dream" speech so eloquently and so brilliantly made clear) remains an absolute necessity in light of the degradations that threaten aggrieved peoples. It is a force registered not only in the opera's dedication to Clarke's mother and to composer D.D. Jackson's mother—"two dreamers of beauty"—but also in the vision at the opera's end of a better, more inclusive world, one where "Our children will be / every colour eyes can know," a world, furthermore, where "states, parents, gods / must have no say." The emphasis here on dream puts me in mind of African-American historian Robin Kelley's recent book, *Freedom Dreams: The Black Radical Imagination*. Addressing "anyone bold enough still to dream" (7), Kelley explains how, from very early in his life, he was taught to "see life as possibility," to imagine "a world where gender and sexual relations could be restructured," or where we could learn to recognize "the poetic and the prophetic in the richness of our daily lives" and "to visualize a more expansive, fluid, 'cosmos-politan' definition of blackness" (2). In like fashion, Clarke's libretto is calling on all dreamers to work towards a more inclusive vision of valued social practices.

Offering an alternative to the doggedly Eurological operatic tradition, *Québécité* marks an unprecedented opportunity on the Canadian operatic stage to generate bold new stagings of identity. Music, like dream, this jazz opera tells us, can empower us (to borrow again from Kelley) to hear "life as possibility." Its power also resides in its ability to foster (and to sustain) vibrant artistic and critical initiatives dedicated to sounding a more inclusive vision of community-building and intellectual stock-taking for the new millennium. And in an era when demands for tighter controls on immigration and border-crossing threaten the dreams of the aggrieved, the structures of hope, possibility, and momentum embodied in Clarke's rainbow quartet of lovers seem particularly pertinent.

Ajay Heble is Professor of English at the University of Guelph and Artistic Director of The Guelph Jazz Festival. He commissioned George Elliott Clarke and composer D.D. Jackson to write Québécité *to be premiered at the tenth anniversary edition of The Guelph Jazz Festival in September 2003.*

WORKS CITED

Clarke, George Elliott. "Introduction." *Eyeing The North Star: Directions in African Canadian Literature.* Ed. George Elliott Clarke. Toronto: McClelland and Stewart, 1997. xi-xxviii.

Kelley, Robin D.G. *Freedom Dreams: The Black Radical Imagination.* Boston: Beacon Press, 2002.

Lipsitz, George. *Dangerous Crossroads: Popular Music, Postmodernism and the Poetics of Place.* London: Verso, 1994.

startle me into breath

BANERJI

Free at last. Free at last.
Vive Québec libre! Free at last.

GALE

Acknowledgements

Fabriquer de la réalité avec de l'imaginaire:
c'est le propre des artistes et des écrivains.
BEAUVOIR

This "libretto" would not exist were it not for various actors and benefactors who put me up to it, or put me up, or put up with me. Their righteous ranks include: Ajay Heble; Julie Hastings; Jane Hastings; The Guelph Jazz Festival; the Laidlaw Foundation; the Canada Council for the Arts; the University of Toronto; Allan Watts; Djanet Sears; Oodei, Atma, and Neeru Beeharry-Panray of Montagne Longue, Sheila and Bhaskar Rughoonundon of Quatre Bornes, and Nathan Ramlugun of Pointe Aux Canonniers, all of Mauritius; and D.D. Jackson. Also instrumental was the joint autobiography of Richard L. Jackson and Lillian Liu Jackson, titled *Love Song and Sorrow* (2001). It is unpublished, but not unsung. The beneficent D.D. Jackson, the magnificent John Fraser, the munificent Andrew Steeves, and the versificent Robert Edison Sandiford imped and moved improvements to this text. Colin Taylor gave it direction. Clare Goulet, Linda Leith, Kaie Kellough and David Widgington gave it a hearing. Wesley Bates saw everything clearly. Much love to the editors of *The New Quarterly* (11.3, 1991), *Dialog* (11.1, 1997), and the publishers of my *Gold Indigoes* (Carolina Wren Press, 2000) for first airing a few of the 'songs.' Thanks also to Austin Clarke, Michael Ondaatje,

Leon Rooke, and Linda and Michael Hutcheon for soul-sustaining, morale-maintaining support. Finally, I laud my most excellent wife, Geeta Paray-Clarke, whose precepts and passions colour every note of these cantos. (As usual, all the false notes and miscues are my dissonances alone.) *Québécité* was drafted in Vancouver, British Columbia; London and Toronto, Ontario; Montebello, Montréal, Ville de Québec, and Pointe-au-Pic, Québec; Halifax, Nova Scotia; Winchester, England; Barcelona, Spain; and Pointe Aux Canonniers, Mauritius—the Afro-Asian nation with the red, blue, yellow, and green rainbow flag—between 2001 and 2003.

Commissioned by The Guelph Jazz Festival in 2001, *Québécité: A Jazz Opera* debuted at the tenth annual Guelph Jazz Festival, in Guelph, Ontario, at the DuMaurier Theatre, River Run Centre, on September 5, 2003.

ORIGINAL CAST

Kiran Ahluwalia	vocals	*Laxmi Bharati*
Dean Bowman	vocals	*Malcolm States*
Yoon Choi	vocals	*Colette Chan*
Haydain Neale	vocals	*Ovide Rimbaud*

MUSICIANS

bass	John Geggie
piano	D.D. Jackson
cello	Peggy Lee
drums	Jean Martin
trumpet	Brad Turner
trumpet (June 2003)	Kevin Turcotte

Composer	D.D. Jackson
Librettist	George Elliott Clarke
Director	Colin Taylor
Designer	Allan Watts
Co-Designer	Andrew Lu
Technical Director	Paul Ord
French Consultant	Frédérique Arroyas
French Editor	Geeta Paray-Clarke

GUELPH JAZZ FESTIVAL

Artistic Director	Ajay Heble
Executive Director	Julie Hastings

A Note on the Author

This book marks George Elliott Clarke's 20th year in print; his debut book, *Saltwater Spirituals and Deeper Blues*, was published in 1983. Since then, Clarke has authored several books of note, including *Whylah Falls* (1990), *Beatrice Chancy* (1999), and *Execution Poems*, which won him a Governor General's Literary Award for poetry in 2001. Clarke's other prizes include the Portia White Prize and the National Magazine Foundation's Gold Award for Poetry. He is currently the E.J. Pratt Professor of Canadian Literature at the University of Toronto.

AUTHOR PHOTO BY GEETA PARAY-CLARKE

A Note on the Type

Galliard was designed by Matthew Carter (b. 1937) and issued by the Mergenthaler Printing Company for photocomposition in 1978. Its crisp and elegant mannerist letterforms are based on the Ascendonica roman and italic letters of the sixteenth-century French punch cutter, Robert Granjon (c. 1513–1590), arguably the greatest punchcutter who ever lived. The digital version used in this book was issued by Carter & Cone in 1997. At one time, type sizes were described using names, not numbers, and *Galliarde* was the French name for the nine-point size, which was called *Bourgeois* by the English and *Galjart* by the Dutch.

 ¶ The first draft of *Québécité: A Jazz Libretto in Three Cantos* appeared in *Canadian Theatre Review*, 112, Fall 2002, 27–45. The third draft of *Québécité: A Jazz Libretto* appeared in *Testifyin': Contemporary African-Canadian Drama*, Volume II, ed. Djanet Sears, Toronto: Playwrights Canada Press, 2003, 215–55. An earlier version of Ajay Heble's postlude also appeared in *Testifyin': Contemporary African-Canadian Drama*. ¶ The characters herein are pure fiction. Where corporate, media, public, or political figures appear, they are mere symbols, signs, ideas, and images. They are *not* "real" in any real way. ¶ Gaspereau Press acknowledges the support of the Canada Council for the Arts and the Nova Scotia Department of Tourism and Culture. ¶ Typeset in Matthew Carter's Galliard types by Andrew Steeves and printed offset by Gary Dunfield at Gaspereau Press, Kentville, Nova Scotia.

6 5 4 3 2

NATIONAL LIBRARY OF CANADA CATALOGUING IN PUBLICATION DATA

Clarke, George Elliott, 1960–
Québécité / George Elliott Clarke.

Poem; basis for the libretto for the opera of the same title by D.D. Jackson.

ISBN 1-894031-74-1
1. Title.

PS8555.L3748Q42 2003 782.1'0268 C2003-903717-7

GASPEREAU PRESS ¶ PRINTERS & PUBLISHERS
ONE CHURCH AVENUE, KENTVILLE, NOVA SCOTIA
CANADA B4N 2M7